DOGGEREL CATHARSIS
AND POETRY

Doggerel Catharsis and Poetry

Marjorie Rine

Library of Congress Control Number: 2006909094
ISBN: Hardcover   978-1-4257-3806-8
               Softcover   978-1-4257-3805-1

This book was printed in the United States of America.

To order additional copies of this book, contact:
Xlibris Corporation
1-888-795-4274
www.Xlibris.com
Orders@Xlibris.com
34188

CONTENTS

LIFE IS NOT ALL BEER AND SKITTLES . . . .

I have written some form of poetry for as long as I can remember—whether it be school work, party invitations, dedicatory addresses or private thoughts. I saved very little of it until about 1994, when the Muse seemed to visit me frequently and I decided to compile my inspirations. I am out of step with modern poetry which does not make use of rhyme and meter. I love working crossword puzzles and decoding cryptograms. The fun of writing poetry is similar to working puzzles—finding the best words within limitations. Frank Lloyd Wright once said that he disliked designing exhibitions because of the free reign given to the architect. He preferred the challenge of working within limitations. I would like to be a serious poet but, invariably, I think of a twist at the end of my efforts which say, 'Don't take yourself so seriously!' That is why I let the reader decide which is doggerel, catharsis or poetry.

Marjorie Rine

THE PROCESS

A pristine page of paper faces me

The juices of creative forces surge

My pen can set a hundred phrases free

Shall it write a paean or a dirge?

I must act at once or lose the urge

For gifts can be withdrawn at any time

Voila! A thought will finally emerge

That gives me the direction of the rhyme

Will this sober sonnet prove that I'm

A poet who is worthy of his craft?

Is the final copy at its prime

Or does it need a twenty-second draft?

Ambition's lure will not corrupt my morals

But I wouldn't mind a few posthumous laurels.

THE SONNET I PERCEIVE

The sonnet I perceive within my mind

Most likely echoes poets of the past

I'd leave the modern movements all behind

And my lot with the ancient rhymers cast

First, three quatrains, a couplet at the last

With measured feet divisible by five

The scope of possibilities is vast

My wish is that the great IAMB survive

From this discipline I would derive

Satisfaction in the knowledge that I care

Enough to write and help to keep alive

An art form that is now becoming rare

Although I understand that he has died

Spenser would be pleased that I have tried.

THE WORDSMAN

Look at the poet. Study his face;

Though present, his mind is in some other place.

So many similes yet to be used,

Words to be welded and tempered and fused

Meters to conquer and forms to embrace;

He lives in a state of poetical grace.

He knows that his gift, even if in its prime,

Is not guaranteed to endure a lifetime,

So, do overlook his eccentricities,

His seeming detachment and failure to please.

He may become mute as a wan wordless mime

And lose his repute as a master of rhyme;

For, talent is meant to be whetted and honed

And not to be taken for granted, but loaned

To him who will nurture it wisely and well

He who perverts it will hear its death knell,

So, Pity the poet when in a decline

And savor his best like a full-bodied wine.

I can't say that I really like travel. I *have* traveled, seven trips to France—mostly southern France. I love *being* there but I do not like *getting* there or all of the preparations that a busy person must make before and after the trip. Oh, to be 'teleported' as they are on STARTREK!

TRAVEL RESERVATIONS

My clothes are not glamorous modish or chic
I never do seem to fit in with the clique

I fraternize freely with nabob or help
I wade in the ocean with algae and kelp

My world-weary luggage has been 'round the bend
My raincoat is obviously an old friend

My jewelry isn't worth taking a chance
A robber would recognize 'fake' at a glance

Whatever I'm wearing, I wish I could toss it
In favor of something at home in the closet

O, how I aspire to be long, lean and lithe
With repartee witty, compelling and blithe

World travel which broadens the mind often slips
Right out of my brain and adheres to my hips

Sometimes I envision a different me
A super sophistical celebrity

When next I embark on a jaunt or a cruise
I won't take a tote bag or athletic shoes

I'll snub all the waiters and turn up my nose
At anyone clad in his everyday clothes

I'll be dressed by Bergdorf (I order by mail—
None ever need know that they had a big sale)

I'll be suave and haughty, my hair in a bun
But I'd like to bet it won't be half the fun.

OH, BOTHER!

I'm off tomorrow on a trip
To seek a warmer clime
Although I'm pale and slightly stale
I should not take the time

For who will feed the cats
And who will take the papers in?
And place them neatly folded
In the blue recycle bin?

And who will take the calls
From my infernal phone machine?
I must not fail to stop the mail
And fill with gasoline

I need to write some checks
For all the bills soon coming due
And notify the church that I'll
Be absent from my pew

I must clean out the 'fridge'
In case of some emergency
The ladies of the Guild would see
And all think ill of me

I fear, next year I'll disappear
And 'hole up' in my room
I'll read a book, refuse to cook
And never touch a broom

I'll disconnect the phone to still
Its irritating beeper
And then pretend that I am gone
A thousand dollars cheaper.

AU SECOURS!

Exhaustion, sheer exhaustion
    Is what I feel today
I just returned on Friday night
    From three short weeks of play

The engine of the jet can still
    Be heard inside my ears
It's three days since I felt the wince
    Of homebound land gears

Three weeks of fun, sometimes with sun
    Deep in the south of France
My brain benumbed and well succumbed
    To travel's idle trance

When, on return, I soon would learn
    The value of my talents
For my departure had completely
    Thrown the world off balance

The loose ends I so carefully
    Had tied before I traveled
In various committees went
    Ungaveled and unraveled

The Harpies have descended
    With the lists I should remember
Of 'musts' to be accomplished
    Between now and late December

And once again I kick myself
    For being acquiescent
And wish my will were stronger
    Than a jejune adolescent

The die is cast, the time is past
    For learning to say 'no'
My guardian angel won't come down
    To take my cause in tow

The race shall end and who will win
    Is anybody's guess
My strength grows thin. My greatest sin
    Is always saying 'yes'.

I remember, as a small child, sitting on the linoleum (with six children carpeting was neither practical nor affordable) and becoming immersed in the sunlight coming in a shaft through the lace curtained window. There were particles swirling through the ray and no one could convince me that they were not fairies dancing in the sunlight. I found that if I squinted my eyes just a little, they became more real. When I was grown, I found comfort in the fact that a small character in the newspaper cartoons was having a similar experience. I have never stopped squinting and seeing magic.

MYTOPIA

I possess a gift my more than ample frame belies
I'm able to reduce my size by squinting both my eyes
I can become so small that I am part of any space
For, my imagination then is firmly locked in place

I gain an easy entry to a snow scene under glass
And execute a slalom on a mini-mountain pass
I kick the glistening snow and sit astride a tilted sled
Trying to remember that the play is in my head

I slip into a crêche not more than seven inches tall
And stand beside the ox and ass within a wooden stall
I dare to touch the tiny Babe and marvel at his presence
Then mingle with the Magi and the awe inspired peasants

I feel the filmy texture of a stark white morning dress
Caught by the brush of Sargent with a delicate finesse
As if I were released from nature's laws by dispensation
As if my gift were that of being part of all creation

I seldom speak to others of this mystic predilection
Lest, seeing me, they rapidly retreat from my direction
But I have had it all my life and would not trade a minute
Of the power of imagery and all the joys within it.

POETIC PARANOIA

I sit in a restaurant all alone
    And wait for a friend to arrive
I feel rather awkward and stiff as a stone
    It's already twelve forty-five

I look at the menu and then at the clock
    I feel like a poor jilted bride
I nibble a pickle fished out of a crock
    And the waiter begins to be snide

Three iced teas, my eyeballs are floating now
    I know the whole menu by heart
The diners around me are raising a brow
    My composure is falling apart

Twenty-five persons are staring
    And looking at me with chagrin
As if I were some kind of herring
    Which didn't belong in the tin

Did I get mixed up on the hour?
    Is this the right restaurant?
Why do my plans go so sour?
    My stomach is growling and gaunt

I've tried to look busy and devil-may-care
    I've powdered my nose once or twice
I looked a lot better when I arrived there
    An hour ago, if precise

Now all eyes turn toward the entry door
    The expected one stands with aplomb
A personage whom one could never ignore
    Saying, 'Dahling, I'm glad you could come'

Sax Fifth Avenue had a giant sale
    I'm terribly sorry I'm late
Then I had to mend a torn fingernail
    And things like that just cannot wait'.

'Oh, I've had a restful time here', I say
    'Just watching the people go by'
Please, God, I know that I have feet of clay,
    Forgive me for that monstrous lie.

Remember the story of 'The Little Red Hen?' I must have been feeling like her When I wrote 'Afterwrath'. I lived in a large house where the family usually gathered on holidays. Perhaps I overdid the preparations for these events but it was out of love (well, 90% love and probably 10% self-aggrandizement) The next day usually found me at home alone while the others were out playing golf, going to sales or exchanging gifts.

AFTERWRATH

December twenty-six—

    Time to un-deck the boughs of holly

For that I need a ladder,

    Wire cutters and a dolly

The trims that looked so festive

    When hung on December one

Are dried out and suggestive

    Of a holiday undone

There is no Noel music

    On the radio to cheer me

And, if the ladder falls,

    There isn't anyone to hear me

With any luck at all

    I'll crawl and call the E.M.S.

And those who didn't deck the hall

    Can clean up all the mess.

I spent one summer reading accounts of the story of King Arthur. I found that the tales differed decidedly though all had arisen from one or two sources. It seems that the story could take almost any direction that one chose to give it. This is the beginning of what was going to be my 'grand epic' but I was called upon to write a play on the subject to be performed by children—which I did and never got back to my 'grand epic'.

Old Merlin, lately of the crystal cave
The self-appointed keeper of a king
Vowed, though he lose his life, that he would save
Fair Arthur, Britain's royal underling
By night he took the infant from its nurse
Igraine the mother pleaded for her child
The sister Morgan offered up a curse
The wizard left them angry and beguiled
Igraine the innocent had been deceived
By Uther with a false identity
Who laid with her and caused her to conceive
By his own lecherous propensity
And Merlin, the accomplice, bore his share
Of guilt for using magic for the deed
That deed at length resulting in an heir
Who, if acknowledged, surely would succeed
King Uther died soon after Arthur's birth
The realm dissolved into a battlefield
Not one successive leader proved his worth
And many were the swords that were annealed
The wizard who was blessed with second sight
And saw time on a plane with all revealed
Knew that Arthur would be killed for spite
If he were not protected and concealed
The master knew the one to whom he could
Consign the child and keep him free from harm
A man courageous, gentle, kind and good
Who wore a noble lineage on his arm
'Sir Ector, by your actions of the past
That surnamed you the king's Trustworthy Knight
The role of fosterfather has been cast
To this child who may be Britain's future light
Guard him with your life and make him strong
Train him to the sword and to the bow
Let him to your family belong
And raise him as a son of yours should go

I shall undertake to guide his mind
Though I shall not be present every day
Like you, make him gentle, good and kind
But brave enough to keep a foe at bay'
Sir Ector said, 'I gladly will receive
This high commission as a sacred trust
From this time on our lives will interweave
And swords alone will never be our thrust
This child and Kaye, my son, are brothers now
They both will suckle at Drucilla's breast
No one will dare to elevate a brow
Or question lineage even in a jest
His safety thus assured, I 'wait the time
When Britain's banners bear a single sign
And troubadours announce aloud in rhyme
That stars and nations evermore align
What wonder if the cradle I now rock
Contains the germination of a seed
As agile as the flitting sparrow-hawk
As mighty as the warriors of his breed'.
'I must away', said Merlin of the mist
'The deed is done and I have played my part
Though I've been called the Great Enigmatist
I have a thoroughgoing human heart
Farewell, my dear Sir Ector, noble prince
Of seven handsome castle battlements
I am content if Arthur bear imprints
Of thy magnific skill and eloquence'.

CHATEAU ON THE PLAINS

It looms up suddenly, I see
Its towers shimmer in the heat;
A building for posterity
A singular, majestic feat.

Six turrets side by side appear
Attaining monumental height.
I can't believe a chateau here
On this flat treeless Kansas site.

I think I see a cavalier
Come galloping in armor fair.
There is someone—he's coming near,
Forsooth, a Kansas farmer there.

On closer look, I ascertain
I've lost my beautiful chateau
An elevator made for grain
Is in its place, where did it go?

To paraphrase a poet who
Was optically unfocused
'Tis distance makes a pretty view,
A hummingbird may be a locust.

THE FIREFLY

In deepest dusk, before the dark
    Obscures the evening skies,
I love to go out in the woods
    And watch the fireflies.

I sit alone upon a bench
    Sometime in mid July
And think how fortunate I am
    To see the firefly.

No coin could ever buy the sight
    Of such a grand display;
Their lightning luminescence
    All too soon will go away.

I think I'm in a fairy land
    And I'm the fairy queen
And all my loyal subjects
    Carry lanterns to be seen.

(I know about biology
    And reproduction, too,
But when one's a romantic,
    One can take a different view.)

'Tis sad, indeed, in just a week
    To have to say goodbye
My subjects will desert me—
    Ah, the feckless firefly!

SWALLOWS

There are swallows in my chimney
     And they sing all summer long.
I fear they're nesting at the top
     Where they do not belong.

My cat sits in the fireplace,
     Frustrated by the sound
And wishes he could join them
     With a single, sooty bound.

They tempt him like a siren
     As a feather flutters down
And settles on his pate just like
     A wispy, weightless crown.

He looks to me for sympathy
     To aid him in his plight,
But I am on the swallows' side
     If it comes to a fight.

I really ought to hire a 'sweep'
     To rid me of these pests;
Instead, I am inclined to keep
     My uninvited guests.

It makes me happy just to hear
     Them twittering away
And 'Muff" can find another sport
     To while away the day.

I have always had one or more cats in my household. I should rephrase that sentence. Their have always been one or more cats in my household. One never *has* a cat. A cat honors one with its presence. Perhaps it is some genetic anomaly which has remained with them since the period when they were worshipped by the Egyptians or, perhaps, human beings are particularly susceptible to their feline bullying, secretly admiring their unmitigated gall.

THE CAT

What a stupifying, fascinating
    Creature is the cat
He carefully selects the place
    That forms his habitat.

He likes a place to call home base
    And keep the upper hand
Some furniture to scratch in case
    He's not fed on demand

He will require some loamy land
    Outside, near the back door
Though, inside, there's a box of sand
    He chooses to ignore

His body rhythm tells him to
    Go out at three a.m.
At four, the howling is your clue
    To let him in again

He's fascinated by the flow
    From any bathroom tap
Although he wouldn't wet a toe
    If I should close the trap

He much prefers to have a home
    Where he's the only pet
He is less likely then to roam
    Or need to see the 'vet'

If he is made secure enough
    He'll sleep upon his back
With all his four legs sticking up
    And no thought of attack

If he should meet a mouse some day
    Most unexpectedly
He'd likely turn and run away
    And leave the mouse to me

He trades his native instinct
    For a posh security
His welfare, then, is linked
    To that of his host family

My cat will not admit that he
    Was anything but free
Will not face the reality
    Of his dependency

We co-exist, my cat and I
    It's hard to say who's boss
I wouldn't even bat an eye
    If he should win the toss.

CATS ARE NOT GRATEFUL

Cats are not grateful
        For their daily bread
They feel it their due
        To be pampered and fed

They schedule their dining
        To suit their own mood
And turn up their noses
        At slightly stale food

When I open cans
        Of a favorite treat
They writhe 'round my ankles
        And nip at my feet

Impatient for service
        From smelling the sauces
They vocalize loudly
        To speed up the process

They sleep anywhere
        In my Tudor interior
And treat *me* as if
        I were somewhat inferior

Though they claim ownership
        They allow me to stay
And I secretly pray
        They will not run away

I have a dear friend, a sculptor, who was asked by a Lebanese family which emigrated to the United States three or four family generations ago and who have been successful business people vocal about their love for this country, to make a sculpture to express their gratitude. The piece of art, cast in bronze, is known as 'The Promise of America'. It is in a place of honor in front of our civic center. The sculptor, Babs Mellor, commissioned me to compose a poem for its dedication.

THE PROMISE OF AMERICA

Share with me
Your life so free
Your longing to succeed

Share with me
Your history
Your independent creed

Share with me
The chance to be
A dweller on your soil

Share with me
Prosperity
Attained by honest toil

Bear with me
And you will see
My eager, willing hand

Dare to be
A legacy
To this, my chosen land

To me, a poem can be inspired by almost anything—a beautiful day, a rhythmic cadence or a phrase overheard. Such is 'Too Clever By Half'. I heard an announcer on television say something about a 'corpulent porpoise' and the phrase would not leave my mind. I couldn't help thinking about the time in elementary school when we budding poets were required to write a nonsense poem. This certainly qualifies.

TOO CLEVER BY HALF

There once was a corpulent porpoise
Whose intellect was said to dwarf us.
    He majored in Latin
    And dwelt in Manhattan,
A life more or less endomorphous.

The aforementioned corpulent porpoise
Disappeared near a Mafia fortress.
    Now, the local police
    Who could not find a piece
Sought a quick writ of habeas corpus.

Later on, they obtained a search warrant
For they feared a crime truly abhorrent
    So they ransacked the villa
    In search of a killa
And weren't any better off for it.

One detective who had no defeat in 'im
Saw that eight dinner plates still had meat in 'em
    This snooper, officious,
    Who sniffed all the dishes,
Said the men of the mob must have eaten 'im.

'The next day, they aborted the mission
The live 'corpus' appeared with contrition
    Saying, 'On the contrary,
    I was at the library
Studying nuclear fishin'

IT'S HUMAN NATURE

Have you ever noticed
    That the traits you hate the most
Are often the same traits
    To which you, yourself are host?

The gossip shrugs indignantly
    When she is talked about
One who peddles influence
    Resents another's clout

A writer says another
    Journalist has lost his knack
He, indeed, will then proceed
    To be a common 'hack'

A woman with excesses
    In the world of the ornate
May say, 'Poor Polly Worthington
    Her vanity is great'

And then, there is the person
    Who is almost always late
Who fumes and walks the floor
    When he is forced to stand and wait

I think they are, subconsciously,
    Aware of this device
But who wants to admit
    That he, perhaps, is less than nice

One should be constantly on guard
    To parry their attack
For there are lots of people pots
    Who call the kettle black

THE MISFIT

There was this friend I used to know
    Who never knew a stranger
Her place in high society
    Was grievously in danger

You never knew with whom she would
    Arrive when you'd invite her
It could be an ambassador
    Or Fearless Joe, the fighter

The labels in her clothing read
    Nieman's or J. C. Penney
And, as for pride of ownership
    I'm sure she hadn't any

She drove an ancient kind of car
    Her Rolls she thought pretentious
She was not loath to change a tire
    And knew her jacks from wrenches

I heard a comment in a group
    The speaker was effusive
'Let's ban her from our social set,
    She's terribly inclusive!'

ONE PATINA, TWO PATINA

My house has seen far better days
      It once was like a showplace
With shiny doors and gleaming floors
      And highly polished staircase

The draperies all fell in folds
      Preset by their designer
The furniture was spanking new
      The rugs were even finer

Now years have come and gone and left
      A genuine patina
That comes from children, dogs and cats
      Which make up home's arena

The sofas have a look we call
      Passé or genteel shabby
Mostly a result of claws
      And spite from my old tabby

The floors are slightly buckled now
      With shallow undulations
Some signs of scuffles, skates and spots
      And other mutilations

The window hangings sag a bit
      And cry out, 'Please retire me'
The lamps which flicker when I read
      All plead, 'Oh, please rewire me'

As for the rugs on which we walk
      They've born up rather well
With cushions tossed upon worn spots
      One really cannot tell

The gentle mist of age has come
      And settled on this dwelling
I should give thought to sprucing up
      A preamble to selling

But, we have grown quite similar
      Though structurally sound
And worn around the edges
      We both need our clocks rewound

REFUGE

When I go to the beauty shop
    I think much less of hair
Than of the fact that no one knows
    That I am hiding there

The telephone rings frequently
    But not for me, you see
And even if I see someone I know
    She won't know me

The curlers in my hair and lack
    Of make-up on my face
Assure my anonymity
    In this most hallowed place

To the Choirmaster—1985

A VIEW FROM THE OTHER
SIDE OF THE CHANCEL

Our leader is appalled
　　　　At inattention at the Mass
He wishes us to make a joyful noise
　　　　No tinkling brass

He accuses us of sloppiness
　　　　And slighting our fermatas
Of cacophonic entrances
　　　　And slumping in our cottas

He hints that we are victims
　　　　Of a spiritual impasse
Too diffident to rise above
　　　　The secular morass

We disappoint him most
　　　　In letting down the Elevation
Our AMEN is too weak to move
　　　　A timid congregation

Our guilt is plain, one sees the pain
　　　　That permeates his face,
But extenuating circumstances
　　　　Mitigate our case . . . .

Though we emulate our Maker
　　　　In most matters circumspect
In music and deportment
　　　　We're more likely to reflect

(I don't mean to be conclusive,
　　　　For, indeed, this too shall pass)
The image of the spectre
　　　　In the organ plexiglass.

(He had taken us to task for all
　　　　The services we'd wrecked
For books that dropped and knees that popped
　　　　As we would genuflect!)

I am a casual gardener. I am not intimidated by a weed here and there. I read and try to garden by logic, but am sorely lacking in 'green thumb'. I mulch. I deadhead. I water. I fertilize. Is it too much to ask that they reward me with an occasional bloom or stand straight up instead of lying on their sides? My garden was featured on a garden tour last summer, but it was only because I had a life sized figure of Van Gogh sitting at his easel in it. Fortunately, he drew attention away from my underperformers. The best garden is always next year's garden.

I MADE MY BED

A bright ball in reflective mood

A compost bin for flower food

A sinuous walk of blocks of slate

A fancy pot without a mate

An ivy-covered redbud trunk

A birdbath rescued from some junk

A pair of concrete children there

Who seem completely unaware

That green has covered all but hair

Tomorrow I shall elevate

The dears if I can bear the weight

A rose misplanted in the shade

I'll move it when I find the spade

Three trellises—slightly askew

Which add but little to the view

But, Oh, the flowers in my bed—

The yellow, purple, blue and red

They do excite my sensuous soul

For I dug every blooming hole!

With apologies to William Wordsworth

FOR WHAT MY WORDS ARE WORTH

My heart does not leap up or thrill
When I behold my daffodils
They sit unvaried much like clones
Resembling old-time telephones

I don't dislike their pretty bloom
It's just that they need too much room
Like guests who bid a bright 'hello'
They very soon become 'de trop'

The blossoms fade and leave behind
Those long green blades that one must bind
And wait and wait 'til bye and bye
They wilt and wither ere they die

And, only then can one begin
To put the summer flowers in.

I suppose that everyone at some time has attempted to write about the four seasons. I actually started to write only about Fall because it is a sad time for me for no particular reason other than it bodes winter. I easily wrote 'Fall' and 'Winter', plodded through 'Spring' and was absolutely inspired with 'Summer'. It was as if I could not write fast enough to get it all down. It was almost frightening. I couldn't help thinking of Ruth Montgomery and her 'automatic writing'. Perhaps Ruth was with me or maybe it was the 'little people'.

Vivaldi, move over!

FALL

It's come again, this time of year
    The one I like the least
When living things are yellowing
    And blossoming has ceased

Some say that there is beauty
    In the ivy on the wall
Which turns from green to reddish
    In the season we call Fall

But when the leaves come down
    From ivied wall and maple tree
I feel this metamorphosis
    Is happening to me

The briskness of the air foretells
    The doom of Summer's reign
And I am sore reminded that
    My cycle is the same

For Nature does demand allegiance
    To consistency
We have no choice but to concede
    Superiority

O, God, please send the early bird
    And let me hear him sing
For winters seem more threatening
    And I do long for Spring

I'm willing to die once with grace
    And lie beneath the pall
But must I die each year
    As I experience the Fall?

WINTER

The sky is overcast today
       The air is cold and gray
Should I expect it otherwise
       This January day?

I'm sure within my brain there lies
       Beneath the cerebrum
A little mechanism
       That reacts to loss of sun

A tiny button-shaped device
       That turns me off and on
In proportion to the garb
       The sun elects to don

Old Sol may feel luxurious
       Wrapped in atmospheric mist
But I with my sun sensor
       Find it hard to co-exist

O, but I do forgive him
       When he sheds his outer wear
Enfolds me with his warmth
       And lifts the cloak of my despair.

SPRING

When lying in the first warm rays of April's sun
A gentle breeze moves playfully on pallid cheeks
It seems that my life once again has just begun
And I put to rest the memory of winter weeks

The seed that has lain dormant now begins to stir
The heart repressed by sorrow glimpses new insight
The darkness and the cold reluctantly defer
To a season made for fragile man's delight

Though Fall and Winter do prolong their session
I can't imagine living in another clime
For I must see the seasons in progression
To know my place in inner space and time

Far better than Spring's winsome warmth and welcome cheer
Is the promise of a new beginning every year.

SUMMER

Oh, glorious summer, fulfillment of spring
With joyous abandon the cardinals sing

Away with restraints and with all winter wraps
Consign to the closet the scarves and the caps
And dance in a gossamer garment of gold
On mats of green carpet by summer unrolled
And revel all night with the wee little folk
Unfraught and unfettered by bonnet or cloak
Delight in your prime for the summer is fleeting
And love with a passionate heart wildly beating
Now frolic without any fear of rebuff
For winter will enter the heart soon enough
So, wring the most joy from your time in the sun
Until the gray sky says the season is done

With studied inflection the cardinals sing
Your summer is over but, ah, there is spring.

O, TO BEE!

I do admire those ladies
Who know how to make a quilt
Who spend their days in cutting, piecing
Free from heavy housework's guilt

How they organize themselves so well
With needle, thread and thimble
So that hours pass before their
Fingertips become less nimble

I envy their precision
As they join their every seam
Making teeny tiny stitches
How they garner my esteem

O, they hang them on their walls
And they put them in their closets
If they're family hand-me-downs
They put them in their safe deposits

And they enter competitions
And win ribbons by the score
With a lovely watercolor
Or a Lady Baltimore

They never miss a meeting
Of the monthly quilting guild
And they seem so well adjusted
And their lives are so fulfilled

(I tried to make a quilt once
It was one of my caprices
It now resides inside a trunk
Still in a hundred pieces

Some day some great-grandchild of mine
May find my quilt and finish it
To add my name just under hers
Perhaps would not diminish it)

So my admiration's boundless
Though, with everything I've said,
I have seldom seen a quilter
Put her quilt upon a bed.

A RIDDLE

HE SPEAKS WITH A BROGUE

Look at you
Buffed and laced
Not a stitch
Has been effaced

         You never have
         To bear the weight
         Or trip the lever
         On the gate
         Or start each step
         Across the street
         Or answer to
         A jiving beat
         Or kick a tin can
         From the grass
         Or look so scuffed
         And middleclass
         You shine above
         Your pristine sole
         But come in second
         On a stroll . . . .

                 I must lead
                 Dear satellite
                 For you are left
                 And *I* am right

WHEN CROSSING A FIELD

When crossing a field of lyriope
I came on an ancient calliope
Its paint, chipped and flaked, indicated that time
Had stolen the beauty possessed in its prime

I turned the old handle just hoping to hear
Some semblance of sound from an earlier year
But, lacking in tone, the air was confined
To the hearing alone in the ear of my mind

A gypsy, perhaps, on a warm moonlit night
For love of a maiden was challenged to fight
The wreck that ensued was not worthy of keeping
Because of the havoc the two Roms were wreaking

Or, maybe, the caravan quickly departed
Pursued by a posse with purpose flint-hearted
From pockets found empty soon after the show
Or ethics found wanting in racy tableaux

Or, what if an Indian out on a spree
Pushed the old instrument into a tree
Taking revenge on a fast talking gypsy
For selling the tonic which rendered him tipsy

I brushed off the dirt which obscured faded printing
And barely made out with the aid of some squinting
'JEFFERSON WASHINGTON: POTIONS AND LOTIONS
SPECIAL CONSULTANT FOR ROMANTIC NOTIONS'

My husband brought home to me a copy of The American Poetry Review. It was a nice gesture, but I could not believe the language going under the heading of poetry. I wrote this poem while musing about it.

FORE!

I wish I could foresee the future
Or, at least forebear
Our forefathers forewarned us
Of the sick foredooming flair
Which permeates the forefront
Of au courant poetry
And gives foretaste of decadence
(Or so it seems to me)
I hope that 'grungy' poetry
Forsooth will run its coarse
Then, I forecast, bards will again
Become a major force.
'Til then, I guess I'm one of those
Foresighted rhyming nerds
Who compromise by sprinkling in
A few fore letter words.

GUESTS

We are guests upon this planet
As all living things are guests
But our sense of being part of it
Has slowly been repressed
Ranking high upon the food chain
Has instilled a thought of guilt
And so we have become detached
And find our world atilt
We don't accept our instincts
Of primordial predications
And place ourselves above the need
Of natural sensations
We, too, are part of nature's plan
We must accept our station
And not react to being man
With auto-flagellation
The earth needs tenderness and care
No thinking one denies
But man is loved by Nature, too
Who readily supplies it.

WORDS FROM A BEAT POET

Free verse is just fine
But is no anodyne
To a poet whose beat
        Is obsessive

Who puzzles in rhyme
And will work overtime
For a measure replete
        And expressive

To write open ended
With some lines extended
To me is a feat
        Well worth shunning

My rhyme is confined
To the words in my mind
And my meter is
        Always running.

OVERBOOKED

Is anyone darker
        Than Dorothy Parker—
Habitual quoiffer
        And chronic put-offer?
She wasted her talent
        On escorts ungallant
Then opted instead
        To have dogs in her bed
The famous 'Round Table'
        Was less fact than fable
While deep in their cups
        They all strained for one-ups
The memories have faded
        For this bunch so jaded
The gifts that they frittered
        Leave readers embittered
So, let's put an end
        To this nostalgic trend
Such effete lionizing
        Is due for downsizing.

ONE COMPLEMENT TOO MANY

How kind, dear Mrs. Buffington
    To ask me in to tea
To have a chance to see your home
    And visit vis a vis

Your china is exquisite
    I love your chandelier
Is that a real Monet
    Above your chiffonier?

They say you are descended
    From an ancient family
A daughter of a daughter
    Of the aristocracy

I must pale by comparison
    Such a poor unlucky girl
Just a cousin of a cousin
    Married to an English earl

The teacakes are delicious
    Do you have foreign cooks?
My pastry chefs are German
    And have written several books

Is this your dear Augusta May?
    The image of her father
Perhaps she will grow out of it
    Unless she wouldn't rather

My dear, it is already four
    I simply must be leaving
The time has gone so quickly
    And it's too late for receiving

Perhaps I'll come again next week
    I've so enjoyed our sitting
I count the minutes until then
    Engagements so permitting

My dear, I shall not be at home
    Our hourlong conversation
Has given so much cause for thought
    I need time for contemplation.

At our house, when I was a child, there was a great deal of competition for the crossword puzzle which came in the Saturday newspaper. As I was number five of six children, I seldom won out until the older siblings had left home. We all loved words. This love was inspired by my mother's love for words. While most families kept magazines in the bathroom for casual reading, we had a dictionary. I can still hear my mother, when asked for a definition of a word, pointing her forefinger in the direction of the bathroom and saying, "Go to Webster!" It was not that she did not know the definition for she was hard to stump, but she wanted us to learn to find it for ourselves. Our copy of Webster had lost its cover before my memory and had a sturdy piece of cardboard hand stitched to the front—a sign of Mother's reverence for it. When READER'S DIGEST did an article about the disease suffered by coal miners, we all had to learn to spell pneumonoultramicroscopicsilicovulcanoconiosis. It may seem like overkill, but I used it for years at school talents shows. This was the time of the Great Depression and we took our entertainment wherever we could find it.

PUZZLING POEM

I must admit that I've become
A fribbling crossword freak
And my vocabulary
Is too lingua in the cheek
While others may find stimulation
Gossiping and such
My mind is more inclined to find
The word for hind in Dutch

I never have a feverish chill
I always have an ague
I know that 'rattus muridae'
Were rampant in the plague
A sley is just a weaver's reed
Of no use in the snow
But probably of some good
In a Turk's seraglio

I never have met Ena
Who became a Spanish queen
But, frequently I read of Ents
Envisioned by Tolkien
For sari, don't apologize
It's fash'nable in Inja
And don't go near a pyrogen
For, likely it will singe ya

Do not light a fogon
If you do not want a fire
It may spread to your ingle
And dislodge a bosky friar
Eruct an uninvited guest
Who engenders ennui
For he may be the cause
Of much ado, din or bruit

This predilection for odd words
I came by from my mater
Who said that if I studied
They would come in handy later
She raised us (all six) by the book
The book by Noah Webster
And if we spoke as other folk
Exceedingly distressed her

So, what with auks and ernes and ternes
And duckbilled platypi
Scups and scads and soles and shads
And ichthyosauri
Our little minds were preconditioned
(That we had been muzzled!)
To sit and opine all day long
Why we're so cross and puzzled

LIFE IS NOT ALL
BEER AND SKITTLES . . . .

CONTRITION AT SIX

Her name was Lois Low
'ow' as in how
She was haughty and mean
She spoke with an impediment
When she said her name
'Hello', I said, 'Ole Sow'
I chuckled at my wit
She ran home to her mother
Who ran home to my mother
'You must kneel down and pray
And ask the Lord's forgiveness
For causing someone pain
And then you must go there
And tell her you are sorry'
I knelt behind the closet door
And prayed, 'there is no health in me'
And promised never anymore
To be a spiteful, sinful wretch

She smirked at my apology
I would much rather
Deal with God

If you live in a world

Only one person wide

Only one person tall

And one person inside

With ambition to be

Only self-gratified

You'll find yourself

Easily identified

By the door to your heart

Which is marked

'Occupied'

ESCAPE ARTIST

When my life seems laced with gloom

I would go back to the womb

Though it may appear psychotic

I'd retreat from the chaotic

To the fluid amniotic

And deliberately succumb

To a tasty bit of thumb

Firmly anchored to my 'mum'

Though you probably reprove me

Please don't surgically remove me

When my faith has proved its worth

I'll be ready for rebirth.

LIFE IS A GIFT

Life is a gift

To be savored and treasured

The length of a life

Doesn't need to be measured

The gift may be something

You always have wanted

Or one which requires you

To face it undaunted

A gift is a thing

Of which you become owner

Accept it and show

Gratitude to the donor

For even a strange gift

That you did not seek

Through tending and nurturing

Can be unique

THE HEAVY HEART

The heavy heart
Of one who grieves
Is often borne alone

And he who feels
The greatest weight
May make the meekest moan

Civility
Gentility
Belie the grief within

Only he
With empathy
Can feel at all akin

Life's tragedies
Are not confined
To death, for we may find

That life itself
The daily grind
Can stultify the mind

The wanting
For your children
The anguish when they hurt

The falling short
Of lofty goals
The 'clash' you don't avert

The unfulfilled
The chances missed
The endless undone 'list'

The mills which grind
The troubled mind
Shall never lack for grist

But loneliness
Is self-imposed
The answer is so plain

The one the prophets
All foretold
Can spare us all the pain

For, if indeed,
We take His yoke
Just as a little child

Our lives and all
The world around
Will become reconciled

Don't under-
Estimate the beauty
Of simplicity

A simple heart
With simple love
Is good theology

It is a rule
Of nature
That the soul in harmony

Will benefit
The most and thrive
E'en mid complexity

And is not Harmony
Another name
For Christ, the King?

Come, join the chorus
Willingly
And let your heart take wing.

Your burdens
Will be lifted,
Conjoined with God, your soul

Will take its place
Through gentle grace
And God and man are whole.

APPENDAGES

Arms
And legs
And excess weight

Folks
Who cling
And irritate

Work
That irks
And lies in wait

Any
Kind of
Racial hate

I
When I
Exaggerate

He
When he
Will complicate

We
When we
Will altercate

Storms
That rage
And don't abate

Love
When given
Much too late.

O DEATH

O Death, please come on kitten's feet

When thou art sent for me

With silken tread beside my bed

Come O so tranquilly

Arouse me just to reaffirm

My reverence for life here

And then enroll my fragile soul

In yet another sphere

On kitten's feet then let us flee

By cover of the night

Exultantly, triumphantly

On to the glorious light

PANIC

Panic is the opposite of faith

The two cannot by logic co-exist

For panic is a devil inspired wraith

Which rushes in when faith has been dismissed

When night brings overwhelming tides of fear

And sleep comes not to ease the burdened mind

Call out for faith and it will reappear

When asked by e'en the least of humankind

This gift so freely given by our Lord

This promise of safekeeping and of rest

This symbol of His love for us outpoured

Must be invoked by personal request

Consider how the lilies are arrayed

And never give up hope or be afraid

I LOVE THE WARMTH

I love the warmth
That 'round me wraps
In late midsummer days

Creation's womb
Lures and entraps
The sun's effulgent rays

Enshrouded in
The essence of
Its amniotic spell

I recognize
The presence of
A pealing Sanctus bell

THESE TEARS

These tears do flow

So niggardly

From eyes that know no sleep

Do well up one drop at a time

But will not let me weep

Inside there is a rushing

River torrent to be freed

A longing for unleashing

And a therapeutic need

But tears that flow

      So niggardly

Are worse than none at all

They neither soothe the psyche

Nor remove the bitter gall

CIVILITY'S CRADLE

As I was on my way to life
A journey scarce begun
I saw as through a smoky glass
Impressions one by one
Not concrete facts of deeds or acts
But various sensations
Recorded in subconscious mind
For later contemplations

And as I grew, on them I drew
To form my moral being
The smoky glass gave way to view
My eyes and mind's eye freeing
At this point in my tender life
I made conscious decisions
Of traits that I would cultivate
And those needing revisions

And so to everyone there is
A time for declaration
Of one's intentions toward one's self
Honor or degradation
Whether one is nurtured
In a hovel or a manor
His decision will be written
On his heart's own banner

RESURRECTION

She died with body badly worn

With tongue from lucid language torn

A far cry from the time when she

Was symbol of all strength to me

The race was run, the funeral done

Her friends departed one by one

I was not able to conclude

My burdened mind and brooding mood

At night, she came to me and said,

'Don't grieve for I am by your bed;

The broken body now is dead,

Don't wallow in despair for me

For I am whole again, you see'

And I have come to set you free'.

(My mother came to me. Whether it was that twilight sleep in which everything seems real or whether it was a miracle, I do not know but it did, indeed, set me free.)

For, he tames, that fetters it in verse . . . . John Donne

THE INVADER

O, vile and ugly murderer
    With filthy, sprawling feet
And arms that grasp a stranglehold
    On everything they meet
What care you for the lives you wreck
    The havoc that you wreak
The bodies that were once so strong
    That your grip renders weak
You entered our house stealthily
    To play your vicious roll
And, like a surly matriarch,
    Assumed complete control
You challenge us to battle
    With a twisted, gnarly grin
You grapple with our lifelong faith
    (But that one you won't win)
I pray some newfound weaponry
    Stays your pernicious ruse
And will portend triumphant end
    To your befouled abuse.

FAULTY TOWER

They say she is a tower where strength resides

(Unmindful of the turmoil underneath)

The stoic facial mask belies and hides

The gentle, inward tears of silent grief

Each day she watches as her loved one dies

Without a hope of quickening or relief

Her faith, half drained, sustains and then supplies

The gentle, inward tears of silent grief

She gladly would have traded if she could

And offered to become the thresher's sheaf

Though God declined, she knew He understood

Her gentle, inward tears of silent grief.

CHILDREN'S CREED

I believe that Jesus Christ,
 Of Mary, Virgin Maid,
Through the Holy Spirit,
 In a lowly manger laid,
Was the one, true Son of God
 Who loved Him tenderly
And sent Him down to us
 To give our lives eternity.
He came to earth to be like man,
 To rescue us from blame.
He asked God to forgive us all
 And He endured our shame.

He suffered under Pilate,
 Then our Lord was crucified.
To fulfill His destiny
 For you and me He died.
He was buried in a borrowed tomb
 Sealed with a heavy stone.
The Roman guards stood watch
 To make sure He was left alone.
He descended into Hell then
 On the third day, He arose
And glory shone about Him
 Even brightening His clothes.

He walked with the Apostles
 And He taught them as a friend
Then gloriously ascended
 To a world that knows no end.
He is sitting at the right hand
 Of His loving Father, God.
He will return to judge the earth
 So tell it out abroad.
He is very God of very God
 And light of every light,
Only son begotten—
 I believe with all my might.

AN ANGLICAN FUNERAL SUITS ME FINE

An Anglican funeral suits me fine
I've been to three this week
They're always calm and dignified
Liturgically unique
My non-A friends think they are 'cold'
(They chitchat ere the service)
The standing and the kneeling—
Such actions make them nervous

They say the name of him residing
In the urn or casket
Would never be revealed if they
Were not compelled to ask it
Exaggeration such as this
Is cleared up in a minute
If they will simply read the leaflet
It's the first name in it

Now, as for me, I don't object
To having my name mentioned
Or listing those I leave behind
Such things are well-intentioned
I'd be displeased and not amused
At eulogy or praise
Or graphics in regard
To my too final last malaise

Some Celtic hymns might be the thing
Communion is a given
To make sure that all so inclined
May properly be shriven
A Psalm—the hundred thirty-ninth
Translated for King James
Read by a voice stentorian
I will not offer names

Of course, St. James will be the place
For my last celebration
But, up to me, I'd rather be
Part of the congregation.

THE ATAVISTS

Bells and kells and mystic spells

    Man expands from dark to light

Sounding knells and fearing hells

    Ignorance inducing fright

Crystal light breaks through the night

    He wakes, his spirit moved

Knowing love and earth's delight

    God created, God approved

Made with heart to be contrite

    Made with soul to be attuned

Man, somehow, lost sight of right

    No longer with his God communed

Bells and kells and mystic spells

    Man commands the dark, not light

Sounding knells, denying hells

    Ignorance inducing fright

HEAR THE TICKING

Hear the ticking of the mantel clock
The passing of the time
See the sweeping of the sparrow hawk
Voracious in his prime

Hear the clatter, clatter, clatter
As the world goes on around
Does it matter, matter, matter
When a soul is homeward bound?

Only this, take time to ponder
Did you love life or deplore it?
Did you make a contribution?
Is the world the better for it?

First, the sweeping of the sickle
Then the swath is tied and bound
Yes, it matter, matter, matters
When a soul is homeward bound.